OLD WINE, BROKEN BOTTLE

OLD WINE, BROKEN BOTTLE

Ari Shavit's Promised Land

NORMAN G. FINKELSTEIN

OR Books
New York · London

© 2014 Norman G. Finkelstein

Published by OR Books, New York and London
Visit our website at **www.orbooks.com**

First printing 2014

All rights reserved. No part of this book may be reproduced
or transmitted in any form or by any means, electronic or
mechanical, including photocopy, recording, or any information
storage retrieval system, without permission in writing from the
publisher, except brief passages for review purposes.

Cataloging-in-Publication data is available from the Library of
  Congress.
A catalog record for this book is available from the British Library.

ISBN 978-1-939293-46-6 paperback
ISBN 978-1-939293-47-3 e-book

This book is set in Amalia. Typeset by Lapiz Digital, Chennai, India.
Printed by BookMobile in the US and CPI Books Ltd in the UK.

To Arwa, Afaf, and Sana

*Three daughters of Palestine,
each a living testament
why Palestine must and will
survive*

TABLE OF CONTENTS

Introduction   11

1/ "If Zionism Was to Be, Lydda Could Not Be"   17

2/ "The Real Israel Is...a Shopping Mall"   29

3/ "For the First Time in History, the Jews Could Have the Ability to Annihilate Other Peoples"   45

4/ "Operation Cast Lead Is an Intelligent, Impressive Operation"   71

Conclusion   81

Acknowledgments   85

Notes   87

But Michal's Israeliness now manifests itself in new ways. Every Thursday at midnight, she stands at the door of Allenby 58. In an extravagant getup, with her provocative mannerisms, she tells the bouncers who to let in and who to turn away, all the while looking for the guy she'll have fun with at dawn. Selection is power, Michal tells me.

—*from* My Promised Land

INTRODUCTION

ONCE UPON A TIME it was a commonplace that Israel's founding entailed the dispossession of the indigenous population. After World War II, Hannah Arendt observed matter-of-factly, "it turned out that the Jewish question, which was considered the only insoluble one, was indeed solved—namely by means of a colonized and then conquered territory.... [T]he solution of the Jewish question merely produced a new category of refugees, the Arabs."[1]

Nonetheless Israel's public relations apparatus managed through repetition to instill the myth that this "new category of refugees" was not the inexorable outcome of colonization and conquest, but instead the result of a circumstantial and incidental event for which Israel bore no culpability. The official Zionist tale alleged that via radio broadcasts, and despite Israeli pleas that the Palestinian population remain in place, neighboring Arab states had instructed Palestinians to flee in order to clear the field for invading Arab armies. Although researchers had already disproved this claim by the early 1960s,[2] it required the industry and pedigree of an Israeli historian to lay it to rest.

In 1986, scholarly US journals published a pair of articles by Israeli historian Benny Morris chronicling the ethnic cleansing of Palestine.[3] In one of them Morris graphically recalled the order given by Prime Minister David Ben-Gurion in July 1948 to expel Lydda's 30,000 Palestinian inhabitants, the "large-scale massacre" of upwards of 250 Palestinians in Lydda that precipitated the expulsion, and the ensuing death march in which scores more Palestinians perished. The next year Morris reported this brutal episode and many others in his landmark study, *The Birth of the Palestinian Refugee Problem, 1947-1949*.[4]

The principal organs of American Jewish opinion ignored at the time unwelcome tidings such as Morris's. *Commentary*, at the right end of the political spectrum, and *The New Republic*, at the center, promulgated an "immaculate conception" version of Zionism, according to which Palestine had been literally empty on the eve of Zionist colonization; Israel's founding entailed no wrong because no native population existed on which to inflict a wrong. *The Nation* magazine, at the left end of the spectrum, was scarcely better, and arguably worse. In 1989 it published an eyewitness account of the events in Lydda by an Israeli "peacenik." He purported that "we never really *conquered* Lydda. Lydda, to put it simply, fled" (emphasis in original); "From the jeeps, soldiers fired indiscriminately in all directions. Here they smashed a windowpane, there they killed a chicken"; "there was really no city to conquer. The whole place, except for [future Palestinian leader] George Habash and his sister and a few others, was empty."

It might be wondered why the *Nation* would publish an article about a nonevent. In fact, "the story I am telling here really begins," according to the peacenik, "at night, [when] those of us who couldn't restrain ourselves would go into the prison compounds to fuck Arab women." Actually, to *rape*, but why get hung up on nuances in a story so irresistibly titillating, of an Israeli *Jew* who, unlike his scrawny American counterparts, gets to copulate with macho abandon? And anyhow, his enviously awestruck American editors and readers could rationalize, as the Israeli did, that "those who couldn't restrain themselves did what they thought the Arabs would have done to them had they won the war."[5] Just as, if men were women, and women men; then women would rape men; ergo, it's okay if men rape women. None of the *Nation*'s house feminists, who periodically erupted in politically correct indignation at the vaguest hint of sexism in the magazine's pages, objected to the Israeli fucker's logic.

Such was the impoverished historical and moral sensibility of American Zionism in its heyday, and even at its enlightened extreme.

But in the three decades that have since elapsed, the unsparing findings of serious scholarship have, willy-nilly, seeped into the consciousness of American Jews. They now know too much: the unvarnished truths displacing the old clichés conflict at all points with their liberal ethos, causing a crisis of Zionist faith.[6] Like the tobacco industry after the Surgeon General's warning in the 1960s, the formidable challenge confronting Zionist true believers is to repackage the old product such that it still sells despite its disquieting contents.

Judging by the response to Israeli journalist Ari Shavit's book, *My Promised Land: The triumph and tragedy of Israel*, published in the US in late 2013,[7] Zionism might yet be (or, be made) a marketable commodity among Jews. Prominent figures in the Jewish establishment across the political spectrum—from the Anti-Defamation League's Abraham Foxman to the *Atlantic*'s Jeffrey Goldberg to the *New York Times*'s Thomas Friedman to the *New Yorker*'s David Remnick—have weighed in with effusive praise. "This is the least tendentious book about Israel I have ever read," the *New Republic*'s Leon Wieseltier enthused on the front page of the *New York Times Book Review*. "It is a Zionist book unblinkered by Zionism.... There is love in *My Promised Land*, but there is no propaganda." Coming from this arch propagandist, who formerly retailed the Palestine-was-empty thesis, such an endorsement does not convince. Nor should it.

My Promised Land does acknowledge many uncomfortable facts about Israeli history and society but, besides love (indeed, a superabundance of it), the book is also shot through with exculpatory propaganda and contradictions. The question is whether Israel can yet again inspire American Jews after Shavit's inspired repackaging of no-longer-evadable facts. The answer is probably no. It both recycles too many shattered myths and confirms too many ugly truths to exhilarate anyone outside the depleting (and aging) ranks of Zion's worshippers.

1/ "IF ZIONISM WAS TO BE, LYDDA COULD NOT BE"

THE DISCURSIVE CRUX of *My Promised Land* comes in the chapter recounting the ethnic cleansing of Lydda. Shavit's telling of how "Zionism obliterates the city of Lydda" mostly echoes Benny Morris's critical findings, from which he then proceeds to extrapolate a bigger two-fold truth, one factual, the other a value judgment. First, what happened in Lydda *had* to happen if Zionism was to triumph:

> The truth is that Zionism could not bear Lydda. From the very beginning there was a substantial contradiction between Zionism and Lydda. If Zionism was to be, Lydda could not be. If Lydda was to be, Zionism could not be.
>
> ...
>
> [T]he conquest of Lydda and the expulsion of Lydda were no accident. They were an inevitable phase of

the Zionist revolution that laid the foundation for the Zionist state. Lydda is an integral and essential part of our story. And when I try to be honest about it, I see that the choice is stark: either reject Zionism because of Lydda, or accept Zionism along with Lydda.[1]

And second, what happened to Lydda, albeit a "tragedy," "human catastrophe" and grounds to be "horrified," *should* have happened because of the greater (Jewish) good that ensued:

> One thing is clear to me: the brigade commander and the military governor were right to get angry at the bleeding-heart Israeli liberals of later years who condemn what they did in Lydda but enjoy the fruits of their deed. I condemn Bulldozer. I reject the sniper. [I.e., Israeli soldiers who committed atrocities.] But I will not damn the brigade commander and the military governor and the training group boys [young kibbutzniks]. On the contrary. If need be, I'll stand by the damned. Because I know that if it wasn't for them, the State of Israel would not have been born. If it wasn't for them, I would not have been born. They did the dirty, filthy work that enables my people, myself, my daughter, and my sons to live.

Insofar as Shavit has put forth what, in the wake of a deluge of damning scholarly revelations, is now being touted as Zionism's best defense, it merits parsing his arguments, both on this point and kindred ones, to see just how well they hold up. If they fall, this would suggest that, short of an existential threat to Israel, American Jewry's growing estrangement from it is irreversible.

SHAVIT IS NOT ALTOGETHER CONSISTENT on why, "If Zionism was to be, Lydda could not be. If Lydda was to be, Zionism could not be." At times he suggests a contingent explanation in which Zionists come off as reacting defensively to events outside their control and therefore ultimately blameless. In this rendering, the Zionists came to Palestine bearing benign intentions—indeed, "while some Palestinians do suffer, many of them benefit considerably as Zionism advances.... Jewish capital, Jewish technology, and Jewish medicine are a blessing to the native population, bringing progress to desperate Palestinian communities." But then, beginning in the mid-1930s, just as "[t]he two peoples of the land are working side by side," Palestinians inexplicably and irrationally explode in murderous rage, as an Islamic fundamentalist preacher's call for an anti-Semitic jihad resonates among them. It was only "[f]rom this moment on"—i.e., in the face of Palestinian violence, and after the British Peel Commission recommended (1937) partitioning Palestine and "transferring" the Palestinians out of the prospective Jewish state—that the Zionist movement began to advocate expulsion.[2] Thus Shavit writes: "What was absolute heresy when Zionism was launched became common opinion when Zionism confronted a rival national movement face-to-face."[3]

But at other points, Shavit posits that a significant Arab presence in Palestine conflicted with the very essence of Zionism, as in "From the very beginning there was a substantial contradiction between Zionism and Lydda." In fact, this thesis comes much closer to the truth: if an ethnic Jewish state was ever to arise, Palestine could not be. "Transfer was inevitable and inbuilt in Zionism," Benny Morris observes,

> because it sought to transform a land which was "Arab" into a "Jewish" state and a Jewish state could not have arisen without a major displacement of Arab population; and because this aim automatically produced resistance among the Arabs which, in turn, persuaded the Yishuv's[4] leaders that a hostile Arab majority or large minority could not remain in place if a Jewish state was to arise or safely endure.[5]

Hence, in the sequence of cause and effect, it was not Palestinian violence that induced the Zionist movement to advocate expulsion but, inversely, the intent of the Zionist movement from its inception to ethnically cleanse Palestine that provoked Palestinian violence. As Morris puts it, "the fear of territorial displacement and dispossession"—a perfectly rational fear, as he demonstrates—"was to be the chief motor of Arab antagonism to Zionism."[6] And as Shavit surely knows, already at the birth of Zionism, the idea of expulsion, far from being an "absolute heresy," was discreetly advocated by, among others, founding father Theodor Herzl.[7]

For one disposed, as Shavit clearly is, to justify Israel's creation at the expense of the indigenous population, the question then boils down to: *How does one excuse ethnic cleansing?* This is quite the challenge for a self-described champion of human rights (more on which presently). To begin with, Shavit reduces it to manageable proportions by contextualizing his response in a narrative wherein the expulsion of Palestine's indigenous population is just not that big a deal. If one didn't know better, between the natives, on the one hand, and the pioneers determined to replace them, on the other, one would surely root—as in pre-enlightened US accounts of the conquest of the West—for the pioneers, as bearers of Progress in an otherwise barren land. Although Shavit waxes perplexed at how the first Zionist settlers could have blinded themselves to the Arabs' presence in Palestine, his supposedly propaganda-free story just barely concedes their existence. In Shavit's telling, Palestine might not have been a "land without a people," but it was also not much more than a land with a few scattered and sickly persons, who obstructed the rugged agents of Jewish renewal. "I am no judge, I am an observer," Shavit declares, but, alas, he observes through the judgmental lens of an unreconstructed European imperialist. Here's a sampling of Shavit's juxtapositions, packed into the book's first 70 pages:

NATIVE	PIONEER
[Visitors] notice the infected eyes of the village women, the scrawny children. And the hustling, the noise, the filth.	In the harsh conditions of this remote Ottoman province, Dr. Yoffe is the champion of progress. His mission is to heal both his patients and his people.
Once again [visitors] are confronted with the misery of the Orient: dark, crooked alleyways, filthy markets, hungry masses.... Young boys look like old men. Disease and despair are everywhere.	Mikveh Yisrael is an oasis of progress. Its fine staff trains the young Jews of Palestine to toil the land in modern ways.... The French-style agriculture it teaches will eventually spread throughout Palestine and make its deserts bloom.
This desolate land is where [Jews] will find refuge.	
Scattered among the fields were deadly marshes in which Anopheles mosquitos bred, infecting most of the local Palestinians with malaria.	[Visitors] are relieved to find [in a Zionist colony] such architecture and such a household and such fine food in this backwater.
[N]ative life meandered as it had for hundreds of years. Still, death was in the air. It lurked low in the poison-green marshes of Palestine.	[The pioneers] will drain the thousand-year-old marshes and muck and malarial scourge and clear the valley for progress.
The waters flow slowly..., as they have for a thousand years. Every so often, water trickles into the ditches that the peasants dig in order to nourish their meager crops. But these waters create the boggy marshes from which rise the poisonous vapors of malaria.... Everything here...is idle—the torpor of an ancient land deep in ancient slumber.	Acre after acre, the marshes give way to fertile fields. Zionist planning, Zionist know-how, and Zionist labor push back the swamps that have cursed the valley for centuries. Malaria is on a dramatic decline.
	The gray, arid wasteland has given way to a rich habitat of flora and fauna.... What the orange grower sees all around him is man-made nature.
The downtrodden villagers wonder...where these [pioneers] came from...to awaken the dormant valley from its thousand-year sleep.	[The Jews] were right to come here and build a home and plant a tree and put down roots. Creating something from nothing.[8]

In Shavit's distillation, even the sheep of these pathetic Palestinians are "gaunt." Meantime, the Zionist pioneers manage, while making the desert bloom, also to peruse Marx, Dostoyevsky and Kropotkin, revel in Beethoven, Bach, and Mendelssohn, and are even green-friendly, as they adopt a "humane and environmentally friendly socialism" (he doesn't say whether they recycle paper and soda bottles). So determined is Shavit to prove the natives' torpid ineptitude and so carried away does he get in his paeans to the resourceful Jewish pioneers that he lapses into bizarre non sequiturs. A chapter begins, "Oranges had been Palestine's trademark for centuries." But by chapter's end, one of Shavit's protagonists "wonders about the mysterious bond between Jews and oranges. Both arrived in Palestine around the same time.... Neither Jews nor oranges could have prospered if the British had not ruled over Palestine." In fact, already in the mid-nineteenth century Palestine's indigenous population practiced "intensive planting" of orange orchards, and "from 1880 until the outbreak of World War I, the acreage for citrus orchards more than quadrupled" while "the number of cases of fruit shipped through Jaffa's port increased more than thirtyfold in the half century before the war, due to the increased acreage and partly as a result of new, more efficient agricultural techniques" (Baruch Kimmerling and Joel S. Migdal).[9]

Moreover Shavit cannot resist a single cliché, no matter how insipid:

> The young men...are indeed new Jews. They are strong, buff, beaming with certainty.... [T]heir fine torsos are proudly on display. They are tanned and muscular; they look like models of revolutionary potency. From the recesses of previous generations' humiliation, manly energy is now bursting. The girls are surprisingly provocative...tantalizing.
>
> ...
>
> The [Zionist] collective also dances and sings. At night, young legs are thrust up in the air. Young hands are bound together. Faces glow, eyes glitter. They dance in circles around a bonfire, as if dance is prayer. They dance as if the act of settling in the valley is of biblical significance.
>
> ...
>
> And as the plows begin to do their work, the Jews return to history and regain their masculinity: as they take on the physical labor of tilling the earth, they transform themselves from object to subject, from passive to active, from victims to sovereigns.... After eighteen hundred years, the Jews have returned to sow the valley. In the communal dining hall, they sing joyfully. They dance through the night, into the light of dawn.

Not since Elie Wiesel set his pen to paper has such execrable prose been wrought.[10]

Of course, the tale would not be complete without Shavit's *Oriental Wisdom 101* insight, channeled through a Zionist citrus farmer "who knows the Arabs, their tongue, and their ways": "[T]he trick with the Arabs was to honor and be honored, to give respect and demand respect." A strict yet benevolent disciplinarian, the orange grower "provides medical and financial assistance. The Arab villagers working in the grove respect [him]. They admire his knowledge, they appreciate his fairness, they dread his master's authority.... They are committed to their work and devoted to their master. And yet the orange grower knows that one day, one day." But, rest assured, the grower can always count on "[o]ne Arab [who] is different from the others" named—could it be otherwise?—"Abed," who "is totally loyal and enjoys the owner's total trust." One waits with bated breath for the Shavit sequel, *Uncle Abed's Cabin*.

It is not to begrudge the Zionist settlers the magnitude of their sacrifices and achievements, which impressed many progressive foreign observers at the time,[11] even on the anti-imperialist Left,[12] to recognize that Shavit has contrived a caricature reminiscent of now largely discredited apologetics from the epoch of Western colonialism. If *My Promised Land* reads a notch better than Leon Uris's *Exodus*, it is only because of the book's knowing detail, and if it has triggered paroxysms of ecstasy among Zionist true believers, it is no doubt because they long for a return to the glory days when *Exodus* made Jews swell with wonder and pride. But those with a liberal sensibility—which means most American Jews—will surely recoil, if only from politically correct unease, at this moth-eaten conjuring of benighted natives inhabiting a wasteland who, wise Providence or inexorable Progress has decreed, must retreat before enterprising Europeans determined to transform malarial marshes into a citadel of Science and Civilization.

When he touts Israel's numberless breakthroughs in science, technology and the arts, Shavit seemingly also lends retrospective justification to Palestinian dispossession. The tacit message is that Palestinians, if left to their own devices, would have produced just another destitute, dreary and despotic Arab state,[13] while the world would have been deprived of Israel's high-tech industries, cutting-edge inventions, and flourishing cultural landscape. The argument is not a new one. In the US's triumphant moment, Theodore Roosevelt averred in his classic *The Winning of the West*:

> It is, indeed, a warped, perverse, and silly morality which would forbid a course of conquest that has turned whole continents into the seats of mighty and flourishing civilized nations. All men

> of sane and wholesome thought must dismiss with impatient contempt the plea that the continents should be reserved for the use of scattered savage tribes, whose life was but a few degrees less meaningless, squalid and ferocious than that of the wild beast with whom they hold joint ownership.[14]

It is impossible to disprove this logic in terms of logic. It is arguable that, had the Europeans not conquered North America, it would still be dotted with teepees, and had Jews not entrenched themselves in Palestine, it would still be comprised of mud huts. The fact remains, however, that even an exiguous notion of human rights and international law—the cornerstones of a liberal outlook, to which so many American Jews subscribe—cannot be reconciled with such a moral calculus. The Shavit mindset is a throwback to another epoch that has been superseded in the West (in enlightened liberal precincts, at any rate, and if only as a protocol, not rooted belief) by one less confident of its civilizational superiority and more tolerant of cultural diversity. Nowadays, it's just not good form to cheer giant bulldozers as they demolish ramshackle dwellings that are home to an indigenous people, forcibly relocated in order to make way for Progress, even if the people are offered accommodations elsewhere (which, it need be remembered, the Palestinians were not) in ultra-modern high-rises.

2/ "THE REAL ISRAEL IS... A SHOPPING MALL"

TO JUSTIFY THE INJUSTICE inflicted on Palestine's indigenous population, Shavit formally invokes the conventional Zionist arguments of greater need and higher justice: Were it not for Israel's founding, Jews would have disappeared both spiritually—because of assimilation—and physically—because of anti-Semitism.

When Shavit asserts that, if not for Israel's founding, "I would not have been born," and that it "enables my people, myself, my daughter, and my sons to live," he in part actually intends, "I would not have been born *as a Jew*," and it "enables my people, myself, my daughter, and my sons to live *as Jews*." Hailing as he does from a distinguished line of British Jews, Shavit speculates that, had his family not settled in Israel, he would today probably be an Oxford don. The problem, as he lays it out, is that, because of unprecedented worldly success, non-Orthodox Jews in the UK and everywhere else in the Western world are assimilating, intermarrying, and consequently as a *people* inexorably disappearing:

> Benign Western civilization destroys non-Orthodox Judaism.... This is why the concentration of non-Orthodox Jews in one place was imperative. And the one place where non-Orthodox Jews could be concentrated was the Land of Israel. So Jaffa was inevitable. We had to save ourselves by building a Jewish national home all around Jaffa.

Valid as Shavit's premises might be, it still defies logic, not to speak of justice, why Palestinians should have paid the, indeed *any*, price, to reverse the effects of a deliberate and altogether voluntary option Jews themselves elected. If it would be wrong, and no doubt an avowedly enlightened secularist such as Shavit would think it wrong, to impose external constraints on Jews—residency, dietary, and personal status laws—in order to preserve their peoplehood, then it must be all the more wrong to use force majeure against an exogenous party in order to preserve Jewish peoplehood.

The ultimate irony is, the Israel that Shavit loves and lauds is not recognizably Jewish. The Zionist movement's seminal years witnessed an ideological clash, the principals of which were Herzl, who conceived a state comprised mostly of Jews but cast in the mold of what was highest and best in European culture,[1] and Ahad Ha'am, who envisaged in Palestine a spiritual center infused with reinvigorated Jewish values.[2] To judge by Shavit's account of the contemporary Israeli scene (or, at any rate, the part of it that he embraces), Ahad Ha'am's vision clearly lost out. It might be true, as Shavit purports, that in the course of Zionist colonization and Israel's founding years, Jews created a secular "Hebrew culture" and "Hebrew identity." Still, it's difficult to make out what was distinctively Jewish, except for revival of the Hebrew language (to which Shavit seemingly attaches slight importance), about Israel's collective Spartan existence back then—which, although according to Shavit, it "sanctified the Bible," had more in common with Bolshevism than the Bible. He himself acknowledges that this Hebrew identity "detached Israelis from the Diaspora, it cut off their Jewish roots, and it left them with no tradition or cultural continuity.... Lost were the depths and riches of the Jewish soul."

In any event, one would be hard-pressed nowadays to find anything Jewish in secular Israeli culture, and Shavit doesn't even try. Quite the opposite. He devotes a cheesy chapter of *Time Out*–like prose to boasting of Israel's torrid nightlife ("The word is out that Tel Aviv is hot. Very hot") and no-holds-barred gay life ("the straights now envy the gays," "it's the gays who are leading now"), the anthem of which is, "Forget the Zionist crap. Forget the Jewish bullshit. It's party time all the time." His book's only points of comparative reference and ranking are the fashionable districts of Western metropolises: "Tel Aviv is now no less exciting than New York," "a music scene...that rivals those of London, Amsterdam, or Paris," "[N]o one ever thought [Sheinkin Street] would become Tel Aviv's SoHo," "Allenby 58 is perhaps the fifth most important club in the world.... DJs and drag queens from all over Europe want to come here.... Allenby 58 is for 1990s Tel Aviv what Studio 54 was for 1970s Manhattan," "at Hauman 17, the outcome is a burst of energy unlike anything seen in London, Paris, or New York," "Tel Aviv's liberal and creative culture is just like New York's," "Before me is an Israeli Central Park on the shores of the Mediterranean, a Hampstead Heath in the Middle East." Contrariwise, Shavit repeatedly expresses disdain for Orthodox Jews (and Palestinian Israelis) as a brake on Israeli society and economy.

For all anyone knows or cares, Israel and Israelis might be, as Shavit proclaims, "astonishing," "a powerhouse of vitality, creativity, and sensuality," "innovative, seductive, and energetic," "awesome," "fascinating, vibrant," "extraordinary...absolutely unique," "exceptionally quick, creative, and audacious...sexy even in the way they work," "hardworking and tireless," "one of the most nimble economies in the West...an extraordinary economic accomplishment," "truly phenomenal...astounding...a unique entrepreneurial spirit...a powerhouse of technological ingenuity...a hub of prosperity," a "mind-boggling success," "something quite incredible...extraordinary...authentic and direct and warm and genuine and sexy...exceptional...remarkable," "creative and passionate and frenzied," "phenomenal...epic." But, as distilled through the secular values he prizes, Israel is also just another narcissistic Western consumer society. Indeed, consider Shavit's own description of the "typical Jewish Israeli city of the third millennium":

> [T]he real Israel is...a shopping mall: cheap, loud, intense and lively.... West Rishon is all about its malls. Consumption is its beating heart. I walk into Cinema City, a gaudy temple of twenty-six theaters that offer Rishon LeZion the California it wishes to be. Along the corridors stand wax figures of Superman, Batman, Charlie Chaplin, Humphrey Bogart. There is Ben and Jerry's ice cream, Domino's pizza, Coca-Cola. Youngsters wearing Diesel jeans and GAP sweatshirts and A&F jackets lug enormous vats of popcorn. Nothing remains of the initial promise of the unique beginning.

A "vibrant Israeli culture"? Perhaps. A vibrant *Jewish* culture? No. The most convincing witness is once again Shavit himself: "In the last third of the twentieth century, Hebrew identity was dulled. In the early years of the twenty-first century, it seems to have disintegrated.... The Israeliness that was once here is not really here anymore. The Hebrew culture...is gone."

The only thing Jewish about Shavit's Israel is its demography. Shavit loves Israel not because it is Jewish but because those who created it are Jews. His is an apotheosis of biological superiority, not cultural uniqueness. Hence, the book's paeans to Israel's "outstanding fertility rate," and its designating the "concentration" of Jews as "the essence of Israel."[3] It is also why wholly assimilated, on-the-make American Jews—the Alan Dershowitzes, Norman Podhoretzes, and Martin Peretzes—came to embrace Israel: not because it was distinctively Jewish, but because it was distinctively *not* Jewish. It confirmed that Jews stood in the front rank of *Western* civilization. Jews had beaten the goyim at their own game, even—especially—in killing non-Westerners. In any event, if the raison d'être of Israel's founding, and its justification for dispossessing Palestinians, was so that Shavit could live a Jewish "inner life," he might just as well have stayed in England and married a *shiksa*.

*

When he declares that, if not for Israel's founding, "my people, myself, my daughter, and my sons" would not be alive today, Shavit also means it literally.

The embryonic Jewish state provided in his telling a safe port of entry during the Nazi holocaust, while since 1948 Israel has offered sanctuary from the ever-latent potential for another outburst of lethal anti-Semitism. The race against time figures as a red thread running through Shavit's depiction of the Zionist conquest of Palestine. Zionist leaders supposedly anticipated, and acted in the foreknowledge of, the destruction of European Jewry. Thus we read: "[T]he Herzl Zionists see...the coming extinction of the Jews"; "There is hardly any time left. In only twenty years, European Jewry will be wiped out"; "[Labor Zionist leader Yitzhak] Tabenkin... believes...the Jewish people are heading for disaster. Twenty years before the Holocaust he feels and breathes the Holocaust daily"; "There is a feeling not only of success but of justice.... Europe is becoming a death trap.... Only a Jewish state in Palestine can save the lives of the millions who are about to die. In 1935, Zionist justice is an absolute universal justice that cannot be refuted.... The racist laws of Nuremberg prove Herzl right...: the great avalanche had begun: European Jewry is about to be decimated." In effect, the fear of a Nazi holocaust serves, in Shavit's account, as a moral alibi for Palestine's ethnic cleansing: if the Zionist movement rode roughshod over the indigenous population, it was only in the hope of averting a far greater crime against the Jews in Europe.

It is a staple of Israeli historiography that the Zionist movement acted with a ruthless urgency born of its unique insight into the impending doom.[4] The constant repetition, however, does not make it true. Zionist ideologues disputed the liberal piety that Europe would eventually accommodate the Jews in its midst. The point is moot. What would have happened to Europe's Jews had Nazism not come along cannot be known. The fact that Jews in postwar Europe have managed to gain acceptance (and much more) doesn't disprove the pessimistic Zionist prognosis. Hitler did after all quantitatively "solve" Europe's "Jewish question," while Holocaust guilt might partly account for Europe's postwar welcoming. Possibly the Zionists were correct that Europe had—in the metaphor of Zionist leader Chaim Weizmann—a "saturation point" for Jews beyond which it couldn't dissolve them and consequently would "react against them."[5] But it is a fiction that Zionists predicted the Nazi holocaust, and acted as ruthlessly as they did in its backward shadow. The Zionist movement did not produce first-rank thinkers,[6] let alone ones gifted with prophetic powers. Herzl, for example, posited that, whereas anti-Semitism would continuously disturb Europe's social order, it would not reach the point of criminally violating it: "it will be hot enough to push the Jews out, but, in a basically liberal world, it can never break the ultimate bonds of decency" (Arthur Hertzberg).[7]

Still, if Zionists did not foretell the Nazi holocaust, it *did* happen. Does this indelible, irreducible fact vindicate Zionism and concomitantly justify Palestine's ethnic cleansing? Cool reflection suggests not. Had a Jewish state existed in Palestine before or during the Nazi holocaust, it could not have provided an answer to a crime of such magnitude. More Jewish lives might have been saved, but the sanguinary balance sheet would not have been substantially altered. Indeed, it was only a historical fluke, as Shavit himself acknowledges, that any Jews survived in Palestine. If the Wehrmacht had not been defeated by the Allies at El Alamein, Jews in Palestine would have suffered a fate not unlike Jews in the Warsaw Ghetto.

It might nonetheless be concluded that, although a Jewish state did not offer an answer to it, still, the Nazi hecatomb did validate the need for a Jewish safe haven: when push came to shove, Jews could not count on anyone except themselves to give sanctuary. "Past experience, particularly during the Second World War," Soviet Foreign Minister Andrei Gromyko memorably told the UN General Assembly in 1947 during the debate on Palestine's fate,

> shows that no western European State was able to provide adequate assistance for the Jewish people in defending its rights and its very existence from

the violence of the Hitlerites and their allies. This is an unpleasant fact, but unfortunately, like all other facts, it must be admitted. The fact that no western European State has been able to ensure the defense of the elementary rights of the Jewish people, and to safeguard it against the violence of the fascist executioners, explains the aspirations of the Jews to establish their own State. It would be unjust not to take this into consideration and to deny the right of the Jewish people to realize this aspiration. It would be unjustifiable to deny this right to the Jewish people, particularly in view of all it has undergone during the Second World War.[8]

Irreproachable as it surely is, this plea on behalf of a Jewish refuge cannot be said to sanction Palestine's ethnic cleansing, which, according to Shavit, premised Israel's creation—"If Zionism was to be, Lydda could not be." Although Gromyko's first preference was the establishment in Palestine of "an independent, dual, democratic, homogeneous Arab-Jewish State...based on equality of rights for the Jewish and Arab populations," he was prepared to countenance, if such an arrangement proved unworkable, the partition of Palestine "into two independent autonomous States, one Jewish and one Arab." But neither the Soviet Union, nor any other state that later signed onto the Partition Resolution, sanctioned the erasure of not only the indigenous population's rights but also their physical presence in the prospective Jewish state. On the contrary, the Partition Resolution explicitly stipulated that the Jewish (like the Arab) state must guarantee "all persons equal and non-discriminatory rights in civil, political, economic and religious matters," and prohibited "discrimination of any kind...on the ground of race, religion, language or sex."[9]

The claim that the Nazi holocaust justifies Israel's creation and the resulting dispossession of Palestinians proves yet more problematic in light of Shavit's depiction of subsequent history. If the Jewish state's raison d'être was to avert another Nazi holocaust, this purpose would appear to be defeated by the fact that, according to him, Israel is daily encumbered by fear of, and its survival has repeatedly been thrown in jeopardy by, a "second Holocaust." "For as long as I can remember," *My Promised Land* begins, "I remember fear." From there on, until its last pages, the book comprises a litany of external perils endangering Israel's population: "Israel is the only nation in the West that is existentially threatened"; "The Jewish state is a frontier oasis surrounded by a desert of threat"; "In May 1967...[s]ome feared a second Holocaust"; "Hundreds or thousands of Israeli civilians might be killed as every site and every home in the Jewish state will be within reach of the rockets of those enraged by Israel's very existence"; "[O]n June 7, 1981...mission impossible was accomplished. One meticulous minute over the target [Iraq's nuclear reactor] had removed the threat of a second Holocaust"; "[O]n September 5, 2007, four F-16 bombers took off for the Syrian nuclear reactor.... Once again, one meticulous moment hovering over the target removed the threat of a second Holocaust"; "Iran is not a Netanyahu bogeyman; it is a real existential threat"; "We dwell under the looming shadow of a smoking volcano." The climactic image of Shavit's book portrays "concentric circles of threat closing in on the Jewish state," including an "Islamic circle" ("A giant circle of a billion and a half Muslims surrounds the Jewish state and threatens its future"), an "Arab circle" ("A wide circle of 370 million Arabs surrounds the Zionist state and threatens its very existence"), and a "Palestinian circle" ("An inner circle of ten million Palestinians threatens Israel's very existence")—and what's yet more ominous, "In recent years, the three circles of threat have merged.... [P]ressure is mounting on Israel's iron wall. An Iranian nuclear bomb, a new wave of Arab hostility, or a Palestinian crisis might bring it down.... [I]t is clear that we are approaching a critical test."

Even allowing for Shavit's hyperbole, fearmongering and sheer propaganda,[10] it would be hard to disagree that, next to the dangers confronting Israel, those hanging over the other constituents of world Jewry pale by comparison. To judge by Shavit's own account, then, the physical safety of Jews would probably have been better secured if a Jewish state had not come into being. It cannot be a coherent argument justifying Palestine's ethnic cleansing that Jews need a state to prevent a "second Holocaust," if, of the many places on the planet where Jews currently reside, the only one where they face such a dire prospect is Israel. Indeed, nowadays Israel has arguably become the principal fomenter of anti-Semitism and menace to the welfare of world Jewry.

Shavit denotes the Nazi holocaust "Zionism's ultimate argument." He recalls that more Jews perished at the Nazi killing field of Babi Yar than "in all of the wars of Israel." After emerging from an Israeli Holocaust memorial's "tunnel of...devastation," Shavit "cannot help but feel proud of Israel. I was born an Israeli and I live as an Israeli and as an Israeli I shall die." Stirring words, for sure, but what exactly do they mean? True, fewer Jews have perished in Israel's wars than at Babi Yar, but fewer Jews still have perished in the diaspora. So, how can the Nazi holocaust be Israel's "ultimate argument"? True, in the state created by Zionism, Shavit can live and die as an Israeli, but by his own admission the secular milieu in which he is ensconced lacks Jewish content. So, how can living and dying as an Israeli vindicate Zionism?

In the book's final pages, Shavit drops any pretense that the state created by Zionism can be justified by reference to it:

> What this nation has to offer is not security or well-being or peace of mind. What it has to offer is the

intensity of life on the edge. The adrenaline rush of living dangerously, living lustfully, living to the extreme.... Bottom line, I think, Zionism was about regenerating Jewish vitality.

It is a weird odyssey that Shavit has traversed from the book's first pages to its last ones. He starts by frankly acknowledging the ethnic cleansing of Palestine's indigenous population by the Zionist movement. He proceeds to justify this crime and Israel's attendant creation in the name of Zionism's supposedly higher justice: to avert the spiritual and physical destruction of Jewry. By the end, he discards these rationales and justifies Israel's existence still in the name of Zionism but on the grounds that Israel has enabled Jews to live "dangerously," "lustfully," "to the extreme" and with "vitality." What any of this has to do with Zionism is anyone's guess (wasn't Zionism supposed to enable Jews to live not "dangerously" but *safely*?), while how it can possibly justify ethnic cleansing simply baffles and bewilders. Was it okay to expel Palestine's indigenous population so that Jews in Tel Aviv could boogie?

The fact is, there is no "ultimate argument" for Zionism, let alone one that justifies ethnic cleansing. Zionist ideology originally possessed a superficial plausibility. A century later, it lies in tatters, nowhere more so than in the pages of Shavit's book. It is improbable that Shavit's Zionist apologia will persuade American Jews. His implicit contention that Palestine's (alleged) backwardness mitigates the fate visited by Zionism on the native population will find little resonance among Jews with a liberal sensibility. The claim that Israel has provided an answer to the spiritual and physical dangers threatening Jews will also not convince. The pleasures one can indulge in Shavit's beloved Tel Aviv do not spring from the "Jewish spirit" and can be indulged on a much grander scale in Manhattan. The notion that Israel provides a refuge against a "second Holocaust" would appear to be the reverse of the truth: nowhere are Jews more endangered than in the Jewish state, which is why so many Israelis have taken out a second passport. American Jews no doubt feel a special bond with Israel, not because of Zionism, however, but because of a primordial connection grounded in blood. They will identify with Israel in moments of existential truth, i.e., if and when Israel's physical survival is at stake, but not much beyond. Israel offers nothing to American Jews that they don't already have in abundance, while a lot of what it does have in abundance—racism, warmongering—leaves American Jews, if not disgusted, at any rate embarrassed.

Israel exists: *that* is its ultimate argument. It is a state like any other state, and has the same rights and obligations as any other state. Yes, it was born in "original sin," which no amount of Zionist apologetics can erase. But most (if not all) states have originated in sin. It would be more prudent if Israelis put behind them, finally, Zionist mumbo jumbo and made reparation for the colossal wrong inflicted on the people of Palestine.

3/ "FOR THE FIRST TIME IN HISTORY, THE JEWS COULD HAVE THE ABILITY TO ANNIHILATE OTHER PEOPLES"

SHAVIT'S POLITICAL ANALYSIS oscillates between boilerplate and the bizarre. He brusquely interrupts interlocutors—formally, *My Promised Land* consists of lengthy interviews conducted by him—with incoherent rants delivered with the gravitas of omniscient Truth. One is reminded of right-wing Zionist leader Vladimir Jabotinsky's aphorism, "That profound mystical rumbling which sounds like thunder but is actually only a snore."[1] What's more revealing, Shavit represents the most enlightened, secular sector of Israeli society. He illustrates in his person just how wide is the chasm separating the mental outlook of even the "best" Israelis from the liberal American Jewish sensibility.

Shavit devotes surprisingly little space to Israel's principal wars, but what he does report is either misleading or plain wrong:

- He notes that in 1956 Israel "won the Sinai campaign" and achieved a "decisive victory." However, he omits the uncontroversial fact that Israel provoked the war with Egypt.[2]
- He notes that "In May 1967 the Egyptian army entered the Sinai desert…, directly threatening the State of Israel," and it was then "feared" that a "Pan-Arab invasion…would crush Israel," although further on he tempers this dire forecast by recalling that the Israeli army "was raring to fight." In fact, neither the Egyptian army nor the combined Arab forces posed a serious danger to Israel, while Egyptian President Gamal Abdel Nasser almost certainly did not intend to attack. The Israeli army's victory, far from "astonishing," was predicted by all US and Israeli intelligence agencies.[3]
- He notes that "On October 6, 1973…, the Egyptian army caught Israel by surprise," and that subsequently "the fighting spirit of the Israeli rank and file rescued the nation from the jaws of defeat," although he also observes in

passing and without elucidation that after the 1973 war "we—rightly—thought Israel had missed the opportunity to prevent war by making peace." In fact, Egyptian President Anwar Sadat had already proposed a formal peace treaty with Israel in 1971 on almost the exact terms that Israel accepted after the 1973 war; for two years prior to the 1973 attack Sadat had threatened war unless Israel negotiated a peaceful settlement; Sadat initiated only a limited military operation in order to break the diplomatic deadlock. Far from making "the Arabs realize they could not take us by force," the 1973 war made *Israel* realize that it couldn't keep Arab land by force.[4]

In a curt phrase Shavit notes that "in 1982...Menachem Begin and Ariel Sharon led Israel to a deceitful and outrageous war in Lebanon." The reality is, Israel was scarcely more justified in launching its other wars. "Israel's war experience," Zeev Maoz, formerly head of the Jaffee Center for Strategic Studies at Tel Aviv University, concludes in his magisterial book, "is a story of folly, recklessness, and self-made traps. None of the wars—with a possible exception of the 1948 War of Independence—was what Israel refers to as *Milhemet Ein Brerah* ('war of necessity'). They were all wars of choice or wars of folly."[5] One would never glean this critical fact from Shavit's book, perhaps because it cannot easily be reconciled with his depiction of Israel as under eternal existential threat from its Arab/Muslim neighbors.

Whereas Shavit makes short shrift of Israel's wars, he devotes a full chapter, respectively, to Israel's nuclear reactor at Dimona and to the alleged Iranian nuclear threat. He would have spared himself embarrassment and his readers a zeppelin's fill of hot air had he stuck to his expertise in Tel Aviv's sultry nightlife.

In a tête-à-tête with the engineer who presided over Dimona's construction, Shavit can barely contain his orgasmic thrill: "one of the greatest strategic feats of the postwar years," "For the first time in history, the Jews could have the ability to annihilate other peoples," "the engineer's audacity knew no limits. Under his command, Israeli scientists, engineers, and technicians developed remarkable know-how," "this enterprise demonstrated Israel's acumen and cunning and wherewithal, surpassing all expectations," "I tell [the engineer] that his accomplishments are almost incomprehensible in scope…. I tell him…we're talking about a stupefying success…the scientific installation produced what no one imagined it could produce: an astonishing capability of mass destruction," "Dimona was astounding in its existence and in its opacity[6]…. Dimona symbolized the best of Israel of the 1960s: the vision, imagination, soberness, daring, tenacity, power, restraint, and resolve." (Shavit notes that "[t]he engineer likes my analysis." How surprising.)

Although Shavit acknowledges that many "Israeli academics and intellectuals" as well as "senior cabinet members and politicians" opposed Prime Minister Ben-Gurion's decision to manufacture an atomic bomb, it doesn't prevent him (or his engineer-interlocutor who presided over Dimona's construction) from pronouncing Israel's acquisition of nuclear weapons an existential necessity: "A bell jar had to be placed over [Israelis] to shield them from the predators that lay in wait"; "It had to be done, so he [i.e., the engineer] did it." The retreat of Western imperial powers from the Middle East in the mid-1950s, Shavit argues, left Israel at the mercy of neighboring Arab states. That's not, however, the whole story behind Israel's nuclear program. Shavit fills in the blanks:

> The expulsion of 1948 necessitated Dimona. Because of those dead villages it was clear that the Palestinians would always pursue us, that they would always want to flatten our own villages. And so it was necessary to create a shield between us and them.... We would not allow the Palestinian tragedy to jeopardize the monumental enterprise designed to end our own tragedy.

It's hard to know which is more ludicrous, the notion that Israel needed nuclear weapons to deter a mortal threat posed by Palestinian refugees, or that solicitude for these refugees could have foiled Israel's nuclear ambitions.

"Dimona enables the inhabitants of the Jewish national home," Shavit concludes, "to live relatively sane and full lives." He further alleges, "Dimona prevented total wars. It brought about peace agreements." The one and only example he conjures is that during the 1973 war

> Israel revealed its nuclear missiles for a brief moment, for Russian and American satellites to photograph, but never seriously considered using them.... The Yom Kippur War proved unequivocally that Dimona was Israel's unseen anchor, an inseparable part of its existence. Without Dimona, Israel was like a lone tamarisk in the desert.

Shavit never makes clear why Israel's awesome conventional arsenal couldn't deter its enemies. It is illuminating at this juncture to juxtapose Shavit's apocalyptic bluster against Maoz's sober balance sheet. Confuting Shavit on *every* point, while basing himself on voluminous evidence, Maoz's major findings are these: (1) The quality of mutual coordination, and quantity of armaments amassed, by neighboring Arab states have never sufficed to jeopardize Israel's existence, while Israel's global strategic position was actually improving when it embarked on the Dimona project[7]; (2) Israel's nuclear arsenal has not deterred Arab states from attacking it, or limited the scope of Arab armed hostilities.[8] In regard to the 1973 attack, "[at] no time" during the key strategy session of the Egyptian war council "did the Israeli nuclear capability come up as a factor. On the other hand, Israeli conventional capability was mentioned repeatedly as a constraint on the Egyptian ability to achieve military success"[9]; (3) It was Israel's conventional, not nuclear, arsenal that induced the Arab world to sue for peace, while it was in "most" cases Israeli, not Arab, intransigence, that blocked consummation of these Arab peace initiatives[10]; and (4) Dimona's critics (including those cited dismissively by Shavit) correctly predicted that Israel's nuclear program would escalate both the conventional and unconventional arms race,[11] while the arms race spurred by Dimona has in turn probably decreased Israel's overall security.[12] It might also be noticed that, whereas Shavit rhapsodizes over Israel's policy of "opacity," Maoz points up its destabilizing and sinister underside, not least that an unacknowledged policy lacks public accountability.[13] The point is not that, on any or all counts, Maoz is right and Shavit wrong, but that Maoz produces layered, substantiated and often brilliant analyses whereas Shavit blows soap bubbles. Although predictable, it still speaks volumes that Israel's cheerleaders consign Maoz to oblivion but go gaga over Shavit.

One of the greatest dangers posed by Dimona is that it will eventually provoke Israel's neighbors into acquiring nuclear weapons. When Shavit puts this obvious point (he thinks it's original) to his interlocutor, the engineer replies that Israel should annihilate them *now*, before it's too late.

> [T]here is only one answer: a preemptive strike. He who comes to kill you, rise up and kill him first.... Strike them with everything we've got. Be proactive now, as he and his colleagues were proactive then. "We cannot sit idly," he bellows. "We cannot wait until one fine spring day a white mushroom cloud rises over what is left of our homes."

The habitually loquacious and combative Shavit stays mute. He does *not* disagree.

Readying to take leave of the engineer, Shavit waxes tragi-poetic that Dimona was the "inevitable outcome" of Israel's creation.

> And I dare say to him that there is a tragedy here. We brought not only water to the Negev but heavy water. We brought not only agricultural modernity

> to the land but nuclear modernity. Because between the Holocaust and revival, between horror and hope, between life and death—we did the colossal deed of Dimona.

"The engineer has had enough," Shavit reports. So has the reader.

If Shavit's chapter on Dimona is a lovefest, his complementary chapter on Iran is a hatefest. The threat posed by a nuclear Islamic Republic not just to Israel but also the rest of humanity apparently surpasses the imaginative powers of the human faculty. Herewith is a sample of the doomsday scenarios Shavit contrives in just the first two pages of the chapter. If Iran went nuclear, "the Middle East would go nuclear, the world order would collapse, and Israel's existence would be in jeopardy." It would enable Iran to "become the new dominant power" in the Middle East and "turn it against the American Empire." Unlike a nuclear Israel, which has "acted in an admirably responsible and restrained manner," Iran armed with a nuke would "seek regional hegemony," "want to see Israel decimated," and "might actually use it or pass it on to others who might do so." It will "force" other Middle East states "to go nuclear and will surround the Jewish state with an unstable multipolar nuclear system," which will make the lives of Israelis "an ongoing nightmare."

It is child's play not just to poke holes in but also turn on their head all of Shavit's propositions. Judging by standard indices such as military prowess, performance and expenditure, size of conventional and nonconventional arsenal, and technological edge, Israel is already, and has been since its birth, the regional hegemon. It might be argued that Israel has aspired to regional dominance in self-defense but it has also undeniably exploited its military superiority in order to launch illegal and unprovoked wars of aggression against its neighbors, which cannot be said of Iran. It might be true that Iran's leadership has directed inflammatory (if ambiguous) rhetoric at Israel, but it is also true that, in violation of Article 2 of the UN Charter and without credible justification under Article 51, Israel has openly and repeatedly threatened to initiate armed hostilities against the Islamic Republic.[14] It is hard to credit Israel's "admirably responsible and restrained" nuclear policy when it has amassed a surfeit of 80 nuclear warheads and has enough plutonium for perhaps 200 nuclear warheads, and also probably possesses tactical (battlefield) nuclear weapons that cannot be reconciled with a professed policy of "last-resort" nuclear deterrence.[15] If Iran now aspires to be a nuclear power, it is—as Iran experts observe,[16] and even neoconservative hawks[17] and Israel's lobbyists in Washington concede[18]—*not* from ideological fervor to annihilate Israel but, on the contrary, from rational calculation to enhance its own security and regional clout. Whatever might ensue among its neighbors if Iran acquires nuclear weapons, Israel's own arsenal already has, if not caused, still spurred Egypt, Syria, Iraq and Iran to acquire weapons of mass destruction, and, however probable it is that Iran will pass nukes to a rogue state in the future (in fact, it's improbable), Israel already facilitated apartheid South Africa's development of them in the past.[19] International public opinion has been as skeptical of Israel's as of Iran's peaceful intentions,[20] while even a pair of Council on Foreign Relations experts conclude that should Washington "fail to prevent Iran from going nuclear, it can contain and mitigate the consequences of Iran's nuclear defiance," if it "acts confidently and wisely to exploit Iran's weaknesses," and *also* signals that it "is willing to work with, rather than against, Iran's legitimate national aspirations."[21]

Shavit doesn't attempt to seriously substantiate any of his claims, let alone refute any of these elementary counterclaims. Instead, he reports on his assignation with another Israeli fanatic (of which that country is not in short supply), former intelligence chief Amos Yadlin. (The "view from [his] balcony is astounding." Is there anything not astounding in Israel?) Shavit informs readers that "Yadlin monitored the situation as the Iranians fooled the International Atomic Energy Agency and fooled the UN and fooled the Western powers, inching closer and closer to their coveted atomic bomb." He goes on to assert that the 2007 US National Intelligence Estimate—according to which, in his sophistic paraphrase, "there was no conclusive evidence that Iran was indeed trying to build a nuclear weapon"[22]—"did not hold water" and that the Americans had also been bamboozled. Shavit knows the whole world was either wrong or lying because Yadlin and his cohorts said so. It never occurs to this faithful servant of the state that perhaps Israeli intelligence, which passed along false information to Washington before the 2003 invasion that Iraq had nuclear weapons,[23] might be using or fooling *him*. (It is also possible, of course, that he's a willing dupe.)

The hero of the hour is naturally Prime Minister Netanyahu ("Enter Benjamin Netanyahu"), who arrives on the scene just in the nick of time to rescue Israel from "some sort of nuclear Auschwitz." His "great contribution," according to Shavit, was to formulate "an effective Israeli military option, and time after time he prepared to use it." It doesn't trouble him that Netanyahu was seemingly prepared to launch an attack that was not only flagrantly illegal but that, by Shavit's own admission, could also have triggered an incalculable and quite possibly catastrophic reaction. (Yadlin's sage opinion, reported approvingly by Shavit, is, "If Israel shied away from taking action just because it was deterred by a few hundred Iranian missiles and a few thousand Hezbollah rockets, it had *no right* and no way to survive.") In fact, however, Netanyahu almost certainly did not formulate such an option because, both militarily and diplomatically, none existed without critical support from Washington, which wasn't forthcoming. But, in the "bluff of the century" (Patrick Cockburn),[24] Netanyahu did *act* in a sufficiently insane fashion—immortalized by the Looney Tunes–like cartoon he displayed during his "grand speech" (Shavit) at the UN—that many countries dreaded he might actually attack if the economic screws on Iran weren't turned yet tighter.

Shavit's one and only regret is that because of missteps by Netanyahu, Israel subsequently lost the political initiative on the international stage. The West failed to do the blessed deed, and as a result the ineluctable burden will yet again fall squarely—*oh, how cruel Fate is!*—on the already overburdened shoulders of the Light Unto the Nations: "If the West does not wake up soon and if America does not show determination, Israel will soon be facing the most dramatic junction. It will be forced to choose between bomb and bombing." Still, even amidst these frightful cogitations, Shavit hopes against hope that "the West will not forsake Israel and will not let it stand alone against the fanatical power wishing to annihilate it." The goal post for Judgment Day keeps moving forward; by chapter's end he puts it at "2013-14." Insofar as Israeli officials have periodically issued warnings since at least as far back as the mid-1990s that Iran is "more dangerous than Nazism because Hitler did not possess a nuclear bomb, whereas the Iranians are trying to perfect a nuclear option" (Shimon Peres),[25] it's a safe bet to take Shavit's latest prediction with a boulder of salt.

Ironically, Shavit also concedes (quoting Yadlin) that, notwithstanding its religious and ideological extremism, Iran's leaders incline towards "strategic prudence" and believe "[t]he future is theirs," and that "[t]hey are not in a hurry, they are not hasty, they make few mistakes." Such an analysis suggests that Israel faces no imminent threat of annihilation. In the meantime, and leaving aside the promising prospects of negotiations with Iran (beginning in late 2013), the obvious way to avert annihilation of *any* state in the region, is—as all reasonable observers agree (Shavit not among them)—transforming the Middle East into a zone free of Weapons of Mass Destruction (WMD). A Nuclear Weapon Free Zone in the Middle East was first proposed in 1974 at the UN by Egypt and Iran. It was modeled after the 1967 treaty establishing a WMD-free zone in Latin America. To date, five such regional zones embracing more than half the states in the international community have been established. A conference to create a WMD-free zone in the Middle East (incorporating all Arab League members, Israel and Iran) was scheduled to convene at the end of 2012, but was torpedoed by the US because of "a deep conceptual gap [that] persists in the region on approaches towards regional security and arms control arrangements."[26] In other words, Israel said no.

A recent proposal carries the distinguished pedigree of the International Panel on Fissile Materials (IPFM), an independent group of arms-control and nonproliferation experts that is cochaired by Professor Frank von Hippel of Princeton University.[27] It calls on both Israel, which "is believed to be the only state in the region that has produced separated plutonium, and possibly highly enriched uranium, the key ingredients in nuclear weapons," and other regional powers to take cautious, transitional steps towards a final agreement with "robust verification." It underscores that "[a]ny effort to make progress towards a Middle East WMD-free zone must reckon with Israel's long standing security concerns," and that "the other countries in the Middle East will have to demonstrate a high level of cooperation and transparency if Israel is to be willing to go all the way to complete, verified nuclear disarmament." It is difficult to gainsay the reasonableness of the IPFM approach, especially when juxtaposed with Shavit's hysterics.

Shavit's infatuation with Israeli nukes, on the one hand, and his obsession with blasting Iran, on the other, place him, in the US political spectrum, not at the left-liberal end, where most American Jews congregate, but snugly among Evangelical Christians on the extreme right. The only thing missing is his prediction of Armageddon in the Holy Land and his being raptured to Heaven.

IF SHAVIT'S REFLECTIONS on Dimona and Iran constitute a recipe for perpetual war, his reflections on the occupation and diplomacy constitute an alibi for not negotiating peace. He skews the historical background and draws unwarranted inferences from the few facts he accurately reports.

Shavit depicts Israel's settlement project as the product of a "rightist fantasy" that was at the outset opposed by the left-wing Labor party. In fact, the historic leaders of Labor laid the foundations of the settlement project right after the 1967 war, not because they were coerced (as Shavit implies) but because, from the occupation's inception, Israel's elite across the political spectrum has been committed to retaining (large swaths of) the Palestinian territories.[28] To this end, left-wing and right-wing governments alike have mobilized a sprawling, complex bureaucratic apparatus and earmarked vast sums of money and resources.[29]

For sure, no love has been lost between the rough-hewn settlers on the West Bank frontier, on the one hand,

and the civilized folk presiding in the Tel Aviv metropolis, on the other. However, such a dialectic has been a commonplace in the annals of colonialism, not least during the conquest of the American West. Although the Federal government looked askance at the encroachments by frontiersmen on Indian land, and although, in the fighting that inevitably ensued, they "speedily sunk almost to the level of their barbarous foes, in point of hideous brutality," Roosevelt recalled in *The Winning of the West*, in the hour of need "the national power was sure to be used in favor of the hard-pressed...wilderness vanguard of the American people." President Andrew Jackson "insisted on the spontaneous, popular character of white expansion," a biographer observed, in order to "obscure the essential role played by...government policy decisions." Although Federal officials displayed "less of cupidity and violence" than the White settlers' local representatives poised on the frontier, Alexis de Tocqueville concluded in his classic *Democracy in America*, both were "equally lacking in good faith," and although on the surface their respective tactics clashed, still, they were "means to the same end."[30] *Plus ça change, plus c'est la même chose.*

Shavit quotes sympathetically the motives espoused by a settlement leader:

> It was about bringing the people of Israel to the mountain of Israel. We would revive Zionism and

> save Israel by climbing up the mountain, by realizing that without a spiritual depth the State of Israel cannot hold. We would revive it through the understanding that the Zionism of the plains is doomed.... We must bring Zionism back to the mountains and bring the mountains back to Zionism.

"I can understand what he says about the plains and the mountains," Shavit knowingly nods. At junctures of such profundity a Polish proverb hastens to mind, "From empty to vacuum." He also puts forth the coruscating thesis that Israeli officials promoted settlement expansion in 1975 because of "fear that what happened in Saigon will happen in Tel Aviv, and that Israel's fate will be similar to that of South Vietnam." Who except Shavit could have discerned a causal nexus between the fall of Saigon and the rise of West Bank settlements?

Shavit deplores one settlement's "militant messianic ideas and...radical school of thought that believed in transforming the land by using unrestrained force," and expresses shock at the settlers' hope that "there will be a great war and the Arabs will vanish." But didn't he himself boldly defend "transforming the land by using unrestrained force" in the course of the 1948 war? Shavit concedes that the "spirit and the modus operandi" of the original Zionist and the West Bank settlers "are remarkably similar," but nonetheless purports that they cannot be compared. Unlike West Bank settlers, he reasons, pre-state Zionists "tried not to cause unnecessary hardship." But didn't he himself describe the ethnic cleansing of Palestine as "an inevitable phase of the Zionist revolution"? A sovereign state could not do in occupied territories, Shavit lectures a settlement leader, "what a revolutionary movement can do in an undefined land." But he himself repeatedly refers to the West Bank as "disputed territory" and "undefined territory." On one page Shavit avers that the settlements "cannot be undone," while a few pages later he speculates that "in the twenty-first century" the settlements "could not be." If, to mangle Emerson, a preposterous inconsistency is the hallmark of great minds, then Shavit must be a veritable genius.

Shavit recycles long-discredited official Israeli propaganda about the "peace process," and supplements it with fantasies of his own invention. He proclaims that Israel offered Palestinians a "grand deal" at Oslo: "a demilitarized Palestine living side by side with a Jewish democratic Israel along the 1967 border." He goes on to quote without demurral the claim of novelist Amos Oz[31] that, by the time of the 1993 Oslo accord, Yitzhak Rabin and Shimon Peres had come around to supporting full Israeli withdrawal from the occupied Palestinian territories ("Not one inch, not one settlement") and "the establishment of a Palestinian state." In the real world, as former Israeli foreign minister Shlomo Ben-Ami reports,

> Rabin was less of a peace architect than some commentators believed him to be.... As a matter of fact, neither Rabin nor, especially, Peres wanted the autonomy [of the Oslo agreement] to usher in a Palestinian state. As late as 1997—that is, four years into the Oslo process when, as the chairman of the Labor Party's Foreign Affairs Committee, I proposed for the first time that the party endorse the idea of a Palestinian state—it was Shimon Peres who most vehemently opposed the idea.... A Palestinian state was clearly not within Rabin's priorities either.[32]

To date, no Israeli government, left, right or center, has come close to agreeing to withdraw from the major Jewish settlement blocs (comprising 10 percent of the West Bank) that preempt the possibility of a viable Palestinian state.

Springing another of his dazzling insights, Shavit alleges that Rabin, Peres and other seasoned Israeli officials negotiating the Oslo agreement were "trapped," "manipulated," and forced to "yield" and "surrender" to Palestinian interlocutors, who "managed to knock [them] to the ground." It's hard to decide which is more absurd, that Yasser Arafat possessed the wile and wherewithal to floor Israel, or that Oslo constituted a trap and defeat not for Palestinians but for Israel.[33]

The political lesson Shavit draws from Palestine's ethnic cleansing is not that Israel must demonstrate compassion in negotiating peace with Palestinians, but that negotiating peace with Palestinians is a fool's errand.[34] He comes reluctantly to the conclusion that they will never reconcile to their dispossession and Israel's creation in 1948:

> When I was a university student I...believed with all my heart in the promise of peace. But only when I turned thirty and began listening seriously to what Palestinians were actually saying did I realize that the promise of peace was unfounded. It played a vital moral role in our lives, but it had no empirical basis.... I worked out a theory. The theory assumed we lived in a tragedy: an almost eternal struggle between two peoples sharing a homeland and fighting over it.... We wanted to believe there was no tragic decree at the heart of our existence. So we had to pretend that it was not by tragic circumstances that our fate was decided, but by our own deeds.... Rather than face a tragic reality imposed on us from without, we chose to create a simplistic narrative of Right against Left.... We created a virtual reality that enables us to

> blame ourselves rather than face the cruel reality we are trapped in.... [T]he Left was somewhat naïve. It counted on a peace partner that was not really there.... Why did the Left cling to this empirically incorrect assumption? Because this assumption enabled it to deny the tragedy of 1948.... [T]he Left endorsed the unsound and irrational belief that ending occupation would bring peace. There was a tendency to see the settlers and settlements as the source of evil and to overlook Palestinian positions that were not occupation-based.... It overlooked the existence of millions of Palestinian refugees whose main concern was not the occupation but a wish to return to their lost Palestine.

Setting aside its incongruous chronology,[35] Israeli leaders, who have come under escalating international pressure in recent years to negotiate a peace agreement, will undoubtedly welcome the Shavit Prophecy. For, its essence is to let Israel politically off the hook: whatever the Jewish state does—whether it builds or doesn't build settlements—and whatever it offers—however reasonable or unreasonable—Palestinians will say no. It is "tragic circumstances" rather than Israeli "deeds" that ultimately account for the political deadlock; ergo, Israel cannot be held accountable if and when the peace process aborts.

The uncontroversial, although frequently ignored and misrepresented, facts are these.[36] A broad consensus anchored in international law has endorsed a two-state settlement of the Israel-Palestine conflict on the 1967 border and a "just" resolution of the Palestinian refugee question. The representative Palestinian institutions have accepted these terms (and put forth principled compromises to take account of political exigencies), whereas Israel has persistently and vehemently rejected them. It might very well be true, as Shavit asserts, that "[t]he underlying wish of a great number of Palestinians is to turn back the political movement that they blame for...turning most of them into refugees." The wonder would be were it otherwise. If, as Zionists claim, Jews still yearned to return from exile after having been expelled from *Eretz Israel* two millennia earlier, it cannot surprise if Palestinians still long to return after being expelled a few decades ago. But does that make a lasting peace impossible? The test will only come *after* the internationally ratified terms of settlement are implemented and will critically hinge on how much good faith and goodwill Israel summons forth to amend for the "tragedy of 1948." It's impossible to predict the outcome with any certainty, however impressive one's prophetic powers.[37] (Judging not by his self-regard but by his track record, Shavit's gifts of prophecy approach zero.[38])

Even a cursory glance at recent history shows that countries and people can change. In the first half of the twentieth century, Germany and Japan probably ranked as the most racist and militarist countries on Earth. Yet, in the annual BBC world surveys, Germany and Japan now top the list of countries said to exercise a beneficent impact on world affairs. In the not-so-distant past, African-Americans were being lynched not in the dead of night but at festive picnic-like occasions.[39] Yet, an African-American has now twice been elected to the highest office in the land, while nowadays African-Americans often prefer the civility of the South to life in the North. If Israel originated in sin, which state didn't? If Israel bears the stigma of "original sin," its fate has nonetheless not been set in stone. It's perhaps impossible to completely transcend the past, at any rate, not until many generations have elapsed, but it's certainly possible to take basic, incremental steps towards achieving a final closure that relegates the past, once and for all, to the past.[40] The pair of essential preconditions for any reconciliation between Palestine's indigenous population and the Jews who displaced them are, on the one hand, Israel's formal acknowledgment of what happened in 1948 and of the obligations that consequently redound on it, and, on the other, its acceptance of the terms ratified by international law and endorsed by nearly the whole of humankind (notably excluding the US) for ending the conflict. Israel has thus far rejected both these preconditions, while the Shavit Prophecy amounts to little more than an excuse for this recalcitrance.

His tragic prediction causes Shavit no end of torment. "The land is cursed," he anguishes. But rather more cursed, one might think, for a Palestinian rotting in a refugee camp, than for Shavit, who can still seek refuge in his "hot, very hot" Tel Aviv discos.

4/ "OPERATION CAST LEAD IS AN INTELLIGENT, IMPRESSIVE OPERATION"

SHAVIT DEPICTS HIMSELF or, at any rate, comes across as a semi-lapsed leftist. In his youth he was a "peacenik," who opposed settlements, supported a Palestinian state, and championed human rights. "Peace was our religion," he nostalgically recalls. Although still considering himself a "left-wing journalist" (he is currently a columnist for *Haaretz*), Shavit has clearly grown skeptical of his past convictions. It's not so much that he has inched, let alone lurched, across the Israeli political spectrum, but rather that the whole Israeli spectrum has shifted to the right, and he has, conveniently, moved right along with it. His personal odyssey (which parallels that of Israeli historian Benny Morris[1]) is thus exemplary of the morphing Israel itself has undergone in recent years, one that has estranged it from the moral universe of American Jews.

Shavit first came to wide public notice during the first intifada when, in 1991, his eloquent account of army service in a Gaza prison camp was published in the prestigious *New York Review of Books*. Reproduced as a chapter in *My Promised Land*, his searing record of Israeli brutality ends on a defiant, black-and-white note: "There are no complexities here, no mitigating circumstances." In an updated addendum to the chapter, however, Shavit discovers and underlines the "complexity" of the situation. Indeed, the notion of *complexity* figures as a leitmotif of the "mature" Shavit:

> Although I always stood for peace and supported the two-state solution, I gradually became aware of the flaws and biases of the peace movement.... [A]s a columnist, I challenge both right-wing and left-wing dogmas.... I have realized that the Israeli condition is extremely complex, perhaps even tragic.

Thus, he muses that the "Israel question" is too "complex" to be grasped by "arguments and counterarguments," and he chastises a veteran left-of-center Israeli politician for having "never accepted the heavy responsibility of dealing with the complexity of Israeli reality." Yet, if as Samuel Johnson famously said, "patriotism is the last refuge of the scoundrel," it might equally

Old Wine, Broken Bottle

be observed, and Shavit's pronouncements on recent developments in Israel tend to confirm, that "complexity" is the last refuge of the apologist.

Shavit remembers the "wave of terror [that] rattled Israel" during the second Palestinian intifada (beginning in 2000), how "Israel was struggling to thwart the suicide bombing offensive," and how the "IDF and the Shin Bet waged a sophisticated and effective counteroffensive." He falls silent however on the fact that, as numerous Israeli and international human rights organizations copiously documented, Israel committed grave human rights violations and war crimes in the course of its "sophisticated and effective counteroffensive," and that the "terror" experienced by Israel paled by comparison.[2]

The "Second Lebanon War" (2006), Shavit reports, "was not a major war. It lasted 33 days and took the lives of 165 Israeli soldiers and civilians and some 1,300 Lebanese, but it never really endangered Israel's existence." Leaving aside the disproportionate 1:8 death ratio (1:20 for civilians), he omits mention of the fact that during the war Israel inflicted massive "deliberate destruction" (Amnesty International) on Lebanese infrastructure, and that it dropped as many as 4.6 million cluster submunitions on south Lebanon, 90 percent of them "over the final three days when Israel knew a settlement was imminent" (Human Rights Watch).[3] On the contrary, the principal concern Shavit registers is that "Israel was not able to defeat" Hezbollah in the war. He ascribes this failure to the deeper defect that "[o]ld-fashioned Israeli masculinity was castrated as we indulged ourselves in the pursuit of absolute justice and absolute pleasure," and that Israel's "youngsters are not willing to kill and get killed." The panacea for "Israel's alarming impotence in 2006," Mr. Macho Man prescribes, is somehow "regaining national potency." But how, pray tell, can Israel get on the road to recovery if "the straights now envy the gays"?

On 27 December 2008, Israel launched an invasion (Operation Cast Lead) that—in the words of Amnesty International—inflicted "22 days of death and destruction" on Gaza. "It feels like hunting season has begun," one Israeli soldier recollected. "Sometimes it reminds me of a PlayStation [computer] game." "You feel like a child playing around with a magnifying glass," another remembered, "burning up ants."[4] The normally voluble Shavit is conspicuously wordless on the Gaza massacre. In *My Promised Land*, that is. During the massacre itself, and before it turned into an Israeli public relations fiasco, you couldn't shut him up. Although Israel had for years imposed an illegal and punishing blockade on Gaza, and precipitated the outbreak of hostilities when it violated a ceasefire with Hamas; and although Israel was committing massive war crimes and crimes against humanity, as it targeted and fired indiscriminately on civilians and civilian infrastructure; and although global public opinion expressed outrage at the protracted massacre against an impoverished, defenseless, caged-in population—notwithstanding, then, that Israel had embarked on a manifestly criminal undertaking, Shavit elected to mount, and to strut manly-like (could it be otherwise?) on, the proscenium stage, day after day, dutifully and fearlessly and energetically, rallying the Nation behind the State and the Leader in its heroic hour, as it booted up the computers and focused laser-like the solar rays on the "ants," and as he, Shavit, cajoled and exhorted, interlarding the official propaganda and lies with tragi-whining pathos, and directing a ferocious fury at the enemy without and, in particular, the enemy within, the handful of Israeli traitors, deserters and shirkers who decried crime where he decreed glory. "Operation Cast Lead is a just campaign," Shavit frothed in one of a succession of *Haaretz* columns.

> Israel-hating Israelis call Operation Cast Lead a war crime. They record the names of each and every Palestinian killed, denounce each and every Israeli action and portray their state as a bully.... While the international community silently understands that a sovereign state is duty-bound to protect its citizens' lives, Israel-hating Israelis believe that

> Israeli lives can be forfeited. While the simple facts indicate that the violence in the south derives from the despicable actions of an extremist organization that turned the Strip into a district of terror, Israel-hating Israelis persist in their hatred of their people and homeland and defend the morality of Hamas' destructive aggression. There is no call for hating the Israel-hating Israelis. At the end of the day, their position is a pathetic one. Their self-righteousness is not at all righteous, and their moralizing has no morality.... Those who blame Israel for everything and exonerate the Palestinians of everything are neither serving the cause of peace nor helping to end the violence and occupation. All they are doing is proving the extent to which they are blinded by their burning self-hatred.

"Operation Cast Lead is an intelligent, impressive operation," he breathlessly continued.

> The coming days will be difficult. There may be errors, perhaps complications, perhaps even victims. But for this very reason now is not the time for a campaign of hate against Israel's leaders, commanders, soldiers and pilots. Just the opposite. This is the time to strengthen the hand of Prime Minister Ehud Olmert, who is proving himself to be a

respected national leader. This is the time to stand behind the commanders, soldiers and pilots working day and night to conduct a difficult, complex and entirely just war. This is the time for Israel to finally behave as a mature nation protecting itself with wisdom and restraint.[5]

How strange that, although he reproduces in his book several of his *Haaretz* columns, Shavit found no space to quote even a single word from one of the many that he churned out during what clearly was his moment in the sun.[6]

In his reconstruction of Israel's ethnic cleansing of Palestine in 1948, Shavit does however suggest the contours of the "complex" morality he now embraces. His words merit repeated quotation:

> One thing is clear to me: the brigade commander and the military governor were right to get angry at the bleeding-heart Israeli liberals of later years who condemn what they did in Lydda but enjoy the fruits of their deed. I condemn Bulldozer. I reject the sniper. But I will not damn the brigade commander and the military governor and the training group boys. On the contrary. If need be, I'll stand by the damned. Because I know that if it wasn't for them, the State of Israel would not have

been born. If it wasn't for them, I would not have been born. They did the dirty, filthy work that enables my people, myself, my daughter, and my sons to live.

Thus, he openly sanctions ethnic cleansing, but with one caveat: "I condemn Bulldozer. I reject the sniper." To judge by his account, what (roughly) separates *Bulldozer* and the *sniper* from the *brigade commander*, *military governor* and *training group boys* is this: on the one side, *Bulldozer* and the *sniper* performed the evil deeds, and come across as coarse and callous, whereas, on the other side, the *brigade commander* and *military governor* issued the orders, and, together with the *training group boys*,[7] exude culture and compassion.

Who can doubt the profundity of a moral calculus that exonerates those giving the orders while holding accountable those who follow them? Who can doubt the profundity of a moral calculus that mitigates a crime because the criminal possesses culture? "Each man at the bar," the Nuremberg Tribunal recalled in its final judgment of the Einsatzgruppen trial,

> has had the benefit of considerable schooling. Eight are lawyers, one [is] a university professor, another a dental physician, still another an expert on art. One, as an opera singer, gave concerts

> throughout Germany before he began his tour of Russia with the Einsatzkommandos.... Another of the defendants, bearing the name illustrious in the world of music, testified that a branch of his family reached back to the creator of the "Unfinished Symphony."[8]

Did the Tribunal err in not granting these refined murderers special dispensation? Who can doubt the profundity of a moral calculus that mitigates a crime because of the defendant's artfully staged humanity? In his infamous Posen speech, Nazi leader Heinrich Himmler extolled the Einsatzgruppen for having stayed human despite the inhuman ordeal Fate had put them through:

> Most of you well know what it means to see a hundred corpses—five hundred—a thousand—lying there. To have gone through this and yet...to have remained decent.... This is a glorious page in our history that has never been written and never shall be written.[9]

Did Himmler and his henchmen deserve early release for having "remained decent"?

The motive behind Shavit's otherwise perplexing categorical bifurcation is not hard to find. For, it's easy to guess on which group Shavit projects himself—*suave, brooding Lieutenant Shavit*—and hence which criminals he exculpates and which he throws to the wolves. It's also a safe bet that Shavit would strike the wonderfully emotive line, "I'll stand by the damned," from his script and not be quite so brash in claiming as his own his forebears' crimes were he actually held accountable in a court of law. It is, finally, ever the marvel how Israelis manage to make themselves look yet more beautiful—*oh, how soulful of Shavit to accept responsibility for foul deeds that everyone knows he, beautiful, cultured Ari, would never commit*—the more criminality they own up to. If the Academy of Motion Picture Arts and Sciences awarded an Oscar for best dramatic performance by a country, Israel would win hands down every year.

CONCLUSION

TRY AS HE DOES to be upbeat about his promised land, Shavit ends the book on an elegiac note.[1] "A movement that got most things right in its early days," he laments, has in recent decades "gotten almost everything wrong." He depicts an Israel, on the one hand, besieged from abroad and fragmented from within, and, on the other, depleted of the mental resolve and moral force to set things right again. In a word, and for all its undeniable achievements, Israel is a mess. Shavit blames everyone around him for this depressing state of affairs. He might better have begun by looking in the mirror. Instead of chastising Israel where chastisement was clearly warranted and before it was too late, Shavit cozied up to power, did its bidding and pilloried those who dared step out of line. In the process he has turned himself into an object deserving only of ridicule: the prophet whose every prediction is wrong, the hack journalist who pictures himself an Oxford don, the macho man who's down with "the gays," the peacenik who preaches perpetual war. Shavit boasts of the "complexity" of his insights. The reality is, they comprise a hardcore of hypocrisy and stupidity overlaid by a tinsel patina of arrogance and pomposity. He's a know-nothing know-it-all who, if ever there were a contest for world's biggest schmuck, would come in second.[2] "My dear friend David Remnick went over the manuscript with his typical professionalism and contributed precious insights," Shavit notes in his acknowledgments. "He is the one who encouraged me to write this book, and he is the one who took care of the book graciously once written." If the *New Yorker* editor were truly his friend, wouldn't he have counseled Disco Ari that he was a little long in the tooth to be out clubbing?

Despite the hosannas showered on *My Promised Land* by the American Jewish establishment, it's unlikely to inspire many American Jews. They already know too much to be fooled, while, notwithstanding his deceits and deceptions, elisions and evasions, even so skillful a propagandist as Shavit can no longer conceal the decay and the downright ugliness. If Israel manages to do the right thing and get its house in order, it will probably exercise a residual, tribal pull on American Jews. If not, it will gradually fade from (or be put out of) their consciousness. But these are trivial considerations by comparison. The bigger question is whether Israel can create a sane society for itself, and leave its neighbors in peace to also establish a normal life. As it happens, many countries confront this challenge, not least the United States. The odds might appear against it, the grounds for pessimism might appear overwhelming. But history is rich in surprises. If the means and ends are just and true, then history also provides ample grounds for hope.

ACKNOWLEDGMENTS

I am indebted to Maren Hackmann-Mahajan for her preternatural editor's eye; to Noam Chomsky, Mirene Ghossein, Abid Qureshi, Jamie Stern-Weiner, Doug Tarnopol, and Cyrus Veeser for comments on an earlier draft; to Rudolph Baldeo, Lee Swanson, and Ron Unz for their friendship and support.

NOTES

INTRODUCTION
1. Hannah Arendt, *The Origins of Totalitarianism* (New York: 1958), p. 290.
2. Norman G. Finkelstein, *Image and Reality of the Israel-Palestine Conflict*, second edition (New York: 2003), p. 57.
3. Benny Morris, "Yosef Weitz and the Transfer Committee, 1948-9," *Middle Eastern Studies* (October 1986); Benny Morris, "Operation Dani and the Palestinian Exodus from Lydda and Ramle in 1948," *Middle East Journal* (Winter 1986).
4. Benny Morris, *The Birth of the Palestinian Refugee Problem, 1947-1949* (Cambridge University Press: 1987). An expanded version of Morris's study was published by Cambridge in 2004 under the title *The Birth of the Palestinian Refugee Problem Revisited*.
5. Amos Kenan, "Four Decades of Blood Vengeance," *Nation* (6 February 1989).
6. Norman G. Finkelstein, *Knowing Too Much: Why the American Jewish romance with Israel is coming to an end* (New York: 2012).
7. Ari Shavit, *My Promised Land: The triumph and tragedy of Israel* (New York: 2013).

CHAPTER ONE
1. Echoing left-wing Zionist ideologue Ber Borochov's "stychic process," Shavit posits the historic inexorability of the Zionist

conquest of Palestine, as in "They looked fate in the eye and did what they had to do." For Borochov's stychic process, see his *Nationalism and the Class Struggle* (Westport, CT: 1972).

2. Shavit mistakenly reports that the Peel Commission recommended "a partition of the land into two nation-states, Jewish and Arab." In fact, the Arab portion of Palestine was to be joined to the Kingdom of Jordan.
3. He likewise implies that the Zionist decision to cleanse Palestine of its indigenous population in 1948 sprang primarily not from ideology but military contingency.
4. *Yishuv* denoted Palestine's Jewish community prior to Israel's founding.
5. Morris, *Birth...Revisited*, p. 60.
6. Benny Morris, *Righteous Victims: A history of the Zionist-Arab conflict, 1881-2001* (New York: 2001), p. 37.
7. Morris, *Birth...Revisited*, p. 41. At one point Shavit concedes that a prominent early Zionist did advocate expulsion, but then enters the caveat that it was "scandalous heresy."
8. Shavit's panorama of post-independence Israel replicates this pattern: "While four hundred evacuated Palestinian villages were demolished, four hundred new Israeli villages shaped the new economy and the new map of Israel.... In accordance with a national master plan devised by the government's leading architects and civil engineers in 1950, Palestine vanished and the modern State of Israel replaced it.... Israel of the 1950s was a state on steroids: more and more people, more and more cities, more and more villages, more and more of everything"; "[T]here are no more wildflower fields..., no nomad Bedouins. Palestine was replaced by...sweaty, bustling cities.... From the freeway I turn right to West Rishon. Until 1985 there was nothing here, only the sand dunes.... For nearly a hundred years nothing changed. But...[a]t the age of one hundred, Zionism proved to be strong and potent. Once again it performed the miracle of something-from-nothing. Another modern Israeli city was born"; "[W]ith a grandiose engineering project [Israel] eliminated the lake, clearing an entire region in which it settled veteran pioneers and new immigrants, replacing a backward Palestine with a modern Israel."

9. Baruch Kimmerling and Joel S. Migdal, *The Palestinian People: A history* (Cambridge: 2003), pp. 14, 462n14.
10. The clichés pour forth with numbing regularity. Of one youthful European refugee who immigrates to Israel and later becomes a prominent academic, Shavit writes: "Only in Israel did he not have to justify himself or hide himself. Only as an Israeli could he turn from being an object of history to being a subject of history. Only as an Israeli could he be the master of his own fate.... Mental agility, physical strength, and fearlessness marked [him] as a son of the land. He had found his place in the world. The haunted boy from the ghetto had become a total Israeli." Of others he writes, "They rapidly shed the past. On the first day they returned from the fields sunburned, and on the second day they returned sunburned, but on the third day they were tanned Israelis."
11. Richard Crossman, *Palestine Mission* (London: 1947). Crossman was a British Labor Party MP.
12. Isaac Deutscher, *The Non-Jewish Jew* (Oxford: 1968), chaps. v-vi. Deutscher, a noted Trotskyist author, became disillusioned with Israel after the 1967 war (see ibid., chap. vii).
13. Shavit laments the lack of appreciation by Israel's Sephardic Jews that it "saved them from...a life of misery and backwardness in an Arab Middle East." Elsewhere he quotes Ehud Barak's description of Israel as "a villa in the jungle," but recoils only at Barak's calling Israel a villa.
14. Theodore Roosevelt, *The Winning of the West* (New York: 1889), v. 4, p. 56.

CHAPTER TWO

1. See his utopian novel *Altneuland* (Haifa: 1961).
2. Of Herzl's *Altneuland*, Ahad Ha'am wrote: "Anyone examining this book will find that in their state the Jews have neither renewed nor added anything of their own. Only what they saw fragmented among the enlightened nations of Europe and America, they imitated and put together in their new land" (Amnon Rubinstein, *The Zionist Dream Revisited* (New York: 1984), p. 13). In a friendly polemic he engaged simultaneously with the renowned Jewish historian Simon Dubnow, who supported cultural autonomy for the Jewish mi-

nority in multinational states, Ahad Ha'am argued, probably correctly, that a state's culture always carries the imprint of its majority nationality and that, consequently, a Jewish spiritual renaissance in a multinational state would be "cribbed and crammed." Simon Dubnow, *Nationalism and History* (Philadelphia: 1958).
3. The flip side is Shavit's dread of Israel's Palestinian birth rate that "endangers the identity of Israel as a Jewish nation-state."
4. See Shabtai Teveth, *Ben-Gurion: The burning ground, 1886-1948* (New York: 1987).
5. Chaim Weizmann, *Trial and Error* (New York: 1949), p. 90.
6. David Vital, *Zionism: The formative years* (Oxford: 1982), p. 348.
7. Arthur Hertzberg, *The Zionist Idea: A historical analysis and reader* (New York: 1977), pp. 50-51. Shavit's account of the Nazi holocaust also lacks subtlety. He reports, "On January 30, 1941, Hitler announces in the Berlin Sports Palace that the outcome of the war will be the annihilation of the Jews." Regarding this same speech, historian Saul Friedländer observes: "instead of explicitly mentioning extermination, he prophesied that the war would 'put an end to Jewry's role in Europe.' His words could have meant complete segregation, deportation—or indeed total extermination" (Saul Friedländer, *Nazi Germany and the Jews, 1939-1945: The years of extermination* (New York: 2007), p. 132).
8. United Nations General Assembly, Seventy-Seventh Plenary Meeting (14 May 1947; A/2/PV.77).
9. United Nations General Assembly, Resolution 181 (II), *Future Government of Palestine* (29 November 1947; A/RES/181(II)).
10. Iraq had not embarked on a nuclear weapons program before Israel's bombing of the OSIRAK reactor in 1981. The Syrian building destroyed by Israel in 2007 was "very likely" a nuclear reactor, but the notion that it posed the "threat of a second Holocaust" speaks more to Shavit's inflamed imagination than reality. Richard Wilson, "Incomplete or Inaccurate Information Can Lead to Tragically Incorrect Decisions to Preempt: The example of OSIRAK," paper presented at Erice, Sicily (18 May 2007, updated 9 February 2008); cf.

Richard Wilson, "A Visit to the Bombed Nuclear Reactor at Tuwaitha, Iraq," *Nature* (31 March 1983), and comments of Wayne White, Former Deputy Director, Near East and South Asia Office, State Department, in "Fifty-third in the Capitol Hill Conference Series on U.S. Middle East Policy" (20 June 2008). Report by the IAEA Director General, *Implementation of the NPT Safeguards Agreement in the Syrian Arab Republic* (30 August 2012).

CHAPTER THREE

1. Vladimir Jabotinsky, *The Jewish War Front* (London: 1940), p. 71.
2. Benny Morris, *Israel's Border Wars, 1949-1956: Arab infiltration, Israeli retaliation, and the countdown to the Suez War* (Oxford: 1997).
3. The scholarly record is surveyed in Finkelstein, *Knowing*, pp. 161-80. Shavit also alleges that Egypt "blockaded the Straits of Tiran." In fact, Nasser quietly lifted the Straits of Tiran blockade shortly after imposing it and proposed international arbitration (rejected by Israel) to resolve the territorial dispute.
4. The scholarly record is surveyed in Finkelstein, *Image*, pp. 150-71.
5. Zeev Maoz, *Defending the Holy Land: A critical analysis of Israel's security and foreign policy* (Ann Arbor: 2006), p. 35.
6. *Opacity* refers to Israel's policy of not officially acknowledging its possession of nuclear weapons. See Avner Cohen, *Israel and the Bomb* (New York: 1999).
7. "There is no evidence to suggest that the Arab rhetoric about the annihilation of the Jewish state was anything more than a pipe dream. The data on Arab military hardware and human and financial defense burdens indicate that at no time since 1948 did the Arabs possess a military or political capability that enabled them to accomplish this mission. All this evidence suggests that, to a large extent, the Israeli nuclear project was superfluous at best." (Maoz, pp. 312-13; cf. ibid., p. 347)
8. "[E]ach time Israel actually invoked its nuclear policy in a context of an international crisis or war, its implied or explicit threats failed to achieve their intended aim," "[I]t was Israeli conventional capability rather than its nuclear ca-

pability that affected Arab calculations and the limitations they imposed on the scope of their attacks." (Ibid., pp. 320, 324-25)

9. Ibid., pp. 321-22.
10. "[I]t was the cumulative impact of Israeli conventional deterrence, rather than Israel's nuclear capabilities, that may help account for the change in the Arab willingness to make peace," "There were...peace initiatives emanating from Syria and Egypt prior to the inception of the nuclear project...in the initial phases of this project...and...after the project reached operational status. The holdout in most of these cases was Israel rather than the Arabs." (Ibid., pp. 327, 355)
11. "[S]ome opponents of the nuclear project...argued that the Israeli nuclear project might ignite a dual-track arms race.... [T]he prediction about a dual—conventional and unconventional—arms race did materialize. The Israeli nuclear project was instrumental both in intensifying the conventional arms race and in provoking a nonconventional arms race." (Ibid., pp. 328-29; cf. ibid., p. 354)
12. "The analysis of the conventional and nonconventional arms race in the region suggests that not only did Israel's nuclear policy have a significant impact on the intensification of this arms race but also that...Israel may have been its chief victim. There is reason to believe that Israel faces more complex security risks in the third millennium than it did in the past; certainly it faces graver challenges than it did prior to the inception of its nuclear adventure." (Ibid., p. 341; cf. ibid., p. 348)
13. Ibid., pp. 343-46, 350-53.
14. Article 2 requires member states to "refrain in their international relations from the *threat* or use of force against the territorial integrity or political independence of any state." Article 51 allows for member states to exercise self-defense only in the event of an "*armed* attack." (my emphases)
15. Maoz, p. 352.
16. Trita Parsi, *Treacherous Alliance: The secret dealings of Israel, Iran and the U.S.* (New Haven: 2007), p. 209.
17. Reuel Marc Gerecht, "Iran: Fundamentalism and reform," in Robert Kagan and William Kristol, eds., *Present Dangers:*

Crisis and opportunity in American foreign and defense policy (San Francisco: 2000), pp. 138-39.

18. Dennis Ross and David Makovsky, *Myths, Illusions and Peace: Finding a new direction for America in the Middle East* (New York: 2009), pp. 179-82.
19. Sasha Polakow-Suransky, *The Unspoken Alliance: Israel's secret relationship with apartheid South Africa* (New York: 2010).
20. A 2003 poll of European opinion named Israel the biggest threat to world peace; a majority of respondents in a 2010 BBC global poll believed that, alongside Iran and Pakistan, Israel exerted a mainly negative influence on world affairs—even North Korea's influence was viewed negatively by fewer respondents; a 2013 BBC global poll found that Israel and Iran posed a comparable threat to world peace. Peter Beaumont, "Israel Outraged as EU Poll Names It a Threat to World Peace," *Guardian* (2 November 2003); *BBC World Service Poll 2010* (18 April 2010); *BBC News World* (30 December 2013; http://www.bbc.co.uk/news/world-25496299).
21. James M. Lindsay and Ray Takeyh, "After Iran Gets the Bomb," *Foreign Affairs* (March/April 2010).
22. The NIE document affirmatively stated: "We judge with high confidence that in fall 2003, Tehran halted its nuclear weapons program" (*Iran: Nuclear intentions and capabilities*).
23. John J. Mearsheimer and Stephen M. Walt, *The Israel Lobby and U.S. Foreign Policy* (New York: 2007), pp. 235-36.
24. Patrick Cockburn, "Netanyahu's Threats to Bomb Iran Have Served Israel—and the US—Very Well," *Independent* (13 May 2012).
25. Arnold Beichman, *Washington Times* (12 March 1996).
26. US Department of State, "2012 Conference on a Middle East Zone Free of Weapons of Mass Destruction" (23 November 2012).
27. Frank N. von Hippel et al., *Fissile Material Controls in the Middle East: Steps toward a Middle East zone free of nuclear weapons and all other weapons of mass destruction* (2013).
28. Avi Raz, *The Bride and the Dowry: Israel, Jordan, and the Palestinians in the aftermath of the June 1967 war* (New Haven: 2012). The title comes from a metaphor attributed to Levi Eshkol, Israel's prime minister at the time of the 1967

war: "The trouble is that the dowry [i.e., land] is followed by a bride [i.e., people] we don't want." According to Israeli "dove" Amos Oz, whom Shavit quotes approvingly, "Labor lions" such as Eshkol had opposed retaining even "one inch" of the West Bank. In reality, however: "What distinguished the so-called moderates from the extremists was their reasonable style, which lacked the fire and brimstone so frequently used by the fervent enthusiasts for Greater Israel. But regardless of their pragmatic attitude and milder rhetoric, these 'moderates'—with Prime Minister Eshkol in the lead—were hardly less passionate about the newly acquired lands." (Raz, p. 272)

29. B'Tselem, *Land Grab: Israel's settlement policy in the West Bank* (2002); B'Tselem, *By Hook and By Crook: Israeli settlement policy in the West Bank* (2010).

30. Roosevelt, v. 5, p. 130; Michael Paul Rogin, *Fathers and Children: Andrew Jackson and the subjugation of the American Indian* (New York: 1975), p. 220; Alexis de Tocqueville, *Democracy in America* (New York: 1969), p. 337.

31. Shavit heaps praise on Oz as "*the* peace prophet...the guru of the peace movement and the chief rabbi of Israel's peace congregation," who (among others) "put up a courageous fight against the folly of the occupation and did all [he] could do to bring about peace" (emphasis in original). For the actual, opportunistic record of Oz and Israel's "Peace Now" movement, see Noam Chomsky, *Fateful Triangle: The United States, Israel and the Palestinians*, updated edition (Boston: 1999).

32. Shlomo Ben-Ami, *Scars of War, Wounds of Peace: The Israeli-Arab tragedy* (New York: 2006), p. 220.

33. In another inversion of reality, Shavit purports that, next to the local Palestinian leadership, "Arafat was no easy matter." In fact, Israel preferred the "flexibility of the PLO delegation" to principled homegrown Palestinian leaders. Ibid., p. 211.

34. Inconsistently, Shavit also suggests that the "chance to reach a comprehensive peace" between Israel and Palestinians (as well as with neighboring Arab states) did once exist, but "[n]ow there is no hope for peace."

35. Shavit, who was born in 1957, says he experienced his epiphany of the impossible peace when he turned 30, in the mid-1980s. But he also reports, "In the 1990s I supported the

establishment of a PLO-led Palestinian state." It's hard to conceive how such a Palestinian state could have come into being except in negotiations with Israel, but Shavit says that by the 1990s he was convinced Palestinians would never accept anything short of the whole of Palestine. In other words, he believed with "all my heart" in both the possibility and impossibility of peace.

36. Finkelstein, *Knowing*, pp. 203-48.
37. One might still contend, as Shavit does, that an Israeli withdrawal from the West Bank would entail major security risks ("if [Israel] does retreat, it might face an Iranian-backed and Islamic Brotherhood–inspired West Bank regime whose missiles could endanger Israel's security"). Even crediting his far-fetched scenario, but also filling in the relevant facts he omits, Shavit's position lacks logic or sense. In lieu of a formal agreement with the Palestinians, and notwithstanding the risks, he appears to advocate unilateral Israeli withdrawal from the West Bank (the "occupation must cease even if peace cannot be reached"). But an Israeli withdrawal formalized in a binding agreement with Palestinians that is based on international law and sanctioned by the international community would surely pose fewer security risks than no agreement at all.
38. "Ari Shavit: Apocalypse now, apocalypse forever," *+972 Magazine* (21 November 2013; http://tinyurl.com/q7lj9e4).
39. Leon F. Litwack, *Trouble in Mind: Black southerners in the age of Jim Crow* (New York: 1998).
40. The same principle applies, mutatis mutandis, regarding Shavit's complementary premonitions that the Arab/Muslim world in general will never accept a Jewish state in its midst.

CHAPTER FOUR

1. Finkelstein, *Knowing*, pp. 253-97. As a columnist, Shavit's closest American analogue is power-worshipping *New York Times* columnist Thomas Friedman. The Birdman of Alcatraz famously studied ornithology while confined in prison and eventually became a recognized authority. Shavit reads, stylistically, as if he were the Friedman of Alcatraz, locked up in solitary for a decade with only Friedman's columns at hand.

2. Norman G. Finkelstein, *Beyond Chutzpah: On the misuse of anti-Semitism and the abuse of history*, first paperback edition (Berkeley: 2008), part II. On a related note, Shavit sings the praises of Aharon Barak, former chief justice of the Israeli Supreme Court ("brilliant liberal jurist...admired worldwide...judiciary genius...one of the most respected jurists in the world"). Yet, Barak and the Court over which he presided played an instrumental role in legitimizing the Israeli occupation's criminality, such as legalizing the use of administrative detention, hostage taking, and torture, as well as construction of the Wall in the West Bank. Ibid., pp. 157, 207-20, 227-70, and esp. David Kretzmer, *The Occupation of Justice: The Supreme Court of Israel and the Occupied Territories* (Albany: 2002).
3. Amnesty International, *Deliberate Destruction or "Collateral Damage"? Israeli attacks on civilian infrastructure* (August 2006); Human Rights Watch, *Flooding South Lebanon: Israel's use of cluster munitions in Lebanon in July and August 2006* (February 2008).
4. Norman G. Finkelstein, *"This Time We Went Too Far": Truth and consequences of the Gaza invasion*, revised and expanded paperback edition (New York: 2011).
5. Ari Shavit, "Israelis Who Blame Israel Are Not Helping the Palestinians," *Haaretz* (1 January 2009).
6. For other revolting specimens from *Haaretz*, see Shavit's "The Decisive Hour" (8 January 2009), "Israel's Victories in Gaza Make Up for Its Failures in Lebanon" (12 January 2009), and "World Cannot, Must Not Condemn Our War on Hamas" (13 January 2009). When international opinion turned violently against Israel, and the invasion was about to end, Shavit abruptly started singing a different, although ultimately just as nauseating, tune; see his "Gaza Op May Be Squeezing Hamas, But It's Destroying Israel's Soul," *Haaretz* (16 January 2009). For a stinging rebuke from one of the "Israel-hating Israelis," see Gideon Levy, "The Time of the Righteous," *Haaretz* (9 January 2009).
7. Although acknowledging that the *training group boys* committed war crimes, Shavit pins the blame on the "damned war [that] turned humans into beasts" (quoting a letter).

8. *Trials of War Criminals before the Nuernberg Military Tribunals* (Washington, DC: n.d.), v. iv, "The Einsatzgruppen Case," p. 500.
9. Joachim Fest, *The Face of the Third Reich: Portraits of the Nazi leadership* (London: 1970), p. 115.

CONCLUSION

1. The obvious comparison is with Jeffrey Goldberg's *Prisoners: A Muslim and a Jew across the Middle East divide* (New York: 2006). The overarching conceit of Goldberg's book, that Palestinians and Israelis are both imprisoned by the conflict, comes from Shavit's 1991 account of the Gaza beach detention camp. For a critique of *Prisoners*, see Finkelstein, *Knowing*, pp. 99-122.
2. Wife: *You're such a schmuck, you're such a schmuck, you're such a schmuck that, if ever there were a contest for world's biggest schmuck, you'd come in second.*
   Husband: *Why second?*
   Wife: *Because you're such a schmuck!*
      (Yiddish joke)

Also from OR Books

KNOWING TOO MUCH
**Why the American Jewish Romance
with Israel is Coming to an End**

Norman G. Finkelstein

ISBN 978-1-935928-77-5 PAPERBACK
ISBN 978-1-935928-78-2 E-BOOK
472 PAGES

"Mr Finkelstein makes this argument crisply and convincingly....
[His] research is certainly thorough. His characterisations, too,
can be brilliant, and he spares nobody."
—THE ECONOMIST

Also from OR Books

WHAT GANDHI SAYS
About Nonviolence, Resistance and Courage

Norman G. Finkelstein

ISBN 978-1-935928-79-9 PAPERBACK
ISBN 978-1-935928-80-5 E-BOOK
100 PAGES

"Many of us believe we know who Gandhi was and what he represented. The truth is something quite different, and important. As Norman said to me when he gave me this tiny volume, you can read it in one sitting. That will be an essential sitting for anyone who is interested in the matter of genuine courage in the pursuit of just goals."

—JULIAN ASSANGE

Also from OR Books

"THIS TIME WE WENT TOO FAR"
Truth and Consequences of the Gaza Invasion

Norman G. Finkelstein

ISBN 978-1-935928-43-0 PAPERBACK
ISBN 978-1-935928-44-7 E-BOOK
343 PAGES

"Exceptional and courageous scholarship.... Despite the changing and widening discourse on the Israeli-Palestinian conflict in the United States that now allows for greater dissent and legitimizes criticism of Israeli policy—something this book also examines in considerable detail—the struggle remains acute. This work, among Finkelstein's many others, remains an essential and critical part of that struggle."
—SARA ROY, *JOURNAL OF PALESTINE STUDIES*

"Better than any other book, '*This Time We Went Too Far*' shows how the massive destruction visited on Gaza was not an accidental byproduct of the Israeli invasion but its barely concealed objective."
—RAJA SHEHADEH, AUTHOR, *PALESTINIAN WALKS*

OR Books
www.orbooks.com